The Day My Kisses Tasted Like Disorder
by Emmanuella Hristova

First Printing: 2018

ISBN 979-8-9868851-0-0

Emmanuella Hristova
Bay Point, CA 94565

Cover art created by Emmanuella Hristova

</break>
Acrylic on canvas

Book design and interior graphics created by Emmanuella Hristova

The preface.

*When the end was the beginning, and
the beginning was the end.*

For Dora; I wish you were here.

June 23rd
In the depth of
winter, the flowers do not
bloom, no fruits
appear, the leaves
fall off, and the tree looks
dead, but deep in the
darkness underneath,
the roots grow
and grow
and
grow.

The beginning.

I guess I should thank you,
because you turned me into a poet.

upon identifying the day
I knew I loved you
the moment I saw you
the second time I came to
visit you in The City and you
were wearing a cerulean button-down
that matched your eyes and you
had just shaved your beard and
I wanted to kiss you, but
not like a nervous first kiss or
a slobbery wet one; but rather,

the kind of peck lovers give to one another
after being together for years and
what they're passing between their lips
is time.

September 21st
upon telling you
The air is cold on the rooftop,
running across my bare shoulders
as I tell you how I feel about you.
My arm presses against yours;
yours doesn't move. I use it
for support. Our bodies pressed
against the cool, gritty concrete
of the wall that keeps us from falling to
our deaths down below.
Your eyes wax, deep and
limpid like
pools of ocean water
that I see into, staring back at me,
as if you're
seeing me for the first time.
I see the fear in your face,
breath clutched
between your lips like a
piece of ice
stuck in your throat.
You're afraid to exhale. _Oh shit, oh shit,
oh shit_, say your eyes.

No shit.

upon telling me

I am sitting in a middle school
classroom at lunchtime when you
tell me you want to kiss me. My
breath stops in my throat. Instantly,
my heart beats faster and faster
like an unhinged train racing down
its tracks. I was hungry before,
I'm not hungry anymore. A heat
rises from the depths of my soul,
steaming the surface of my cheeks,
pouring out over the tops of my breasts,
and spilling out in between my thighs.
I flush. My flesh heats up, unable
to contain the fireworks exploding on
the inside of my heart.
He wants to kiss me.

And these explosions going off inside me I imagine will be bolder, brighter, and more beautiful when you finally do.

September 22nd

I remember the first time you tell me
I'm pretty. We are in the kitchen; I'm
running my hands under the cool water
of the sink—water washing me before
I begin my day. The mascara is
heavy on my lashes, my lips pink,
smelling like plastic pigments, the kinds
you haven't tasted on me yet. My
hair spills down my neck because
I go to sleep with it wet and in the
morning wake up with crinkles.
My arms cloaked in magenta chiffon,
soft like strawberries on my skin,
framing the cream a-line dress
that blossoms on my body.
It hugs my breasts, cinches my waist, and
falls at the equator of my thighs.
You appear at my side, mouth perpendicular to
my ear, your pants billowing above
the ground, puffing like pastries, popping like
popcorn as your heels
bounce up and down,
the gaze of
your ice-blue eyes
reaching the ceiling.
You look really pretty, you nod
and tell me before you
bounce away, back to where you
came from,

**and I wonder
why it's taken you
so many months to tell me.**

September 24th

I know you loved me when you
messaged me when I was in
New York, 2,668.57 miles away
from home. While I was sitting in my
sister's oncologist's office,
500 mL of sodium chloride
pumping through her veins
like poison trying to flush out
another poison, and you told me you
missed me and
were thinking of me.

I know you loved me when
I told you my sister had cancer,
and your eyes grew ample
and opalescent like the sky an hour
after dawn, as you sat and listened to
how sad I was.

I know you loved me when
you sat with me on
my bed for two hours, waiting for
the safe cover of nightfall to
sneak on the adjacent construction site
after I
had just come out of the
shower and looked at you with
my bare eyelashes wondering what you
would think of me now that I
had washed the artificial beauty off
my face.
But you crossed your legs
with me, all the while scanning my
naked skin as if searching for
imperfections you could not find,
and your lips spread wide to

smile at me the same way
you do everyday and
your pupils rose like
helium balloons because
you loved me,
and have loved me
for many untold months.

I know you loved me when I
lay next to you in your bed,
cloaked in your plaid pajamas,
my head nestled next to yours on
your pillow as I told you what
your friendship meant to me.
You put your hand to your heart and
told me what a great honor it was,
then grew quiet as your eyes
touched the ceiling and didn't shut
for some time, and you didn't sleep
even though you
were tired.

I know you loved me because you
didn't touch me that night but you
lay next to me softly, azure wide-open
glimpses watching me gingerly
close mine as you
thought about how you loved
me, but didn't know how to tell me, as I
thought about how I loved you, but
didn't know
how to tell you.

I wonder if you/I ever will.

9

upon meaning
Time and distance are the biggest deterrents of love, but they are also its biggest justifiers.

September 29th
It's almost as if you
don't believe
I'm real, like I'm
a doll you marvel at
that's come to life just for you.
A real live woman with
beauty and depth, and a
brain you like to pick,
and a body you like to look at and
touch. A real live woman that
breathes and
thinks and has
feelings for you.
You tell me that you
love to see me, and
talk to me, and
touch me
almost as if
you can't believe I'm real.
You moon over me with
steadfast stares dreaming about
thawing stars, as if I'm
an apparition that will dissolve away;
every time you
break your gaze you wish you could
look at me longer.
You touch me with
tender fingers as if
I'm going to melt away under
your fingertips, as if I'm
going to retreat back into my
paper box,
cloaked in cellophane, tucked away,
untouchable, unreachable.
I pinch you.
You're not
dreaming.
11

upon success

America is a weird place where
we leave the
people we love to
pursue little green pieces of
paper and ink to
fill empty slots on
our resumes.

The middle.

It was sweetest here.

October 5th
Your goodbye kisses are my favorite.
They're soft and sweet, like a crisp bite
from a ripe apple, where the juice
spills down the side of the grainy
flesh, running alongside the

taut skin, **succulent and always
leaving me wanting more.**

October 7th
You've never given me reason not to
trust you. Except for the time you
pinned me down beneath you,
kissing me hungrily as if
my lips were an aged wine casket you've
waited years to pry open and taste
and it was only our
first date.
You had already finished half a
bottle of wine and no one was home in
my apartment.
When you brought up sex I
felt threatened, but when I
didn't respond you
continued to cover me with your kisses
as if nothing had happened.
You had reached into the
very depths of me,
pulling out the tangled
black and white mesh of my dark,
sexual conflicts that colonize my mind
and my heart.

The inexpression of my internal sexuality spilled out to my lips and my kisses tasted like disorder.

I have never felt so in danger
and so safe
at the same time. And I
didn't know if it was
because of you, or
because of me. I

15

fear there's
a crack in this trust that I
just can't seem to shake.

</break>
Acrylic on canvas

17

I hesitate when you kiss me because I am afraid you will taste the disaster brewing underneath my skin.

Or maybe, my kisses taste hot, like a dangerous sun storm raging on the broiling surface of our most familiar star. Or maybe, they taste cool, like a bubble rising to the surface above a deep ocean cavern that holds fountains of dark chaos beneath its depths. Or maybe, they taste fluid, like running the edges of worn book pages across your lips, inhaling the texture of clandestine paper and ink that spill out unknown stories. Or maybe, you kiss me because you are sucking out the poison that penetrates from the cocoon of my heart, pulsing through abysmal channels till it reaches the contours of my fingertips. You probably feel it like a heat on your skin, like an electric stove growing too searing to tolerate. Or maybe, you kiss me because you like the taste of disorder; to you it tastes sweet. To me it feels like catastrophe.

October 17th

the beginning of the end

Alcohol gives you enough courage to
ask me about sex. Even though,
we've only been officially dating
for less than
three weeks. Even though, you
rarely tell me that you
think I'm pretty, even though, you've
never picked me flowers, or taken me to
dinner or introduced me to
anyone as your girlfriend. Even though,
you've never brought me home to
your parents. Even though,
you've never told me you
love me.
I convinced myself you
were different
because you were my best friend and a
feminist, and you
had never touched me or
come on to me during our
friendship.
But now that I
let you kiss me,
you won't stop
touching me or
coming on to me.
That letting my lips touch yours
was a contract I signed
without reading the fine print: participant
subject to hasty sexual advances
without warning.
The care you took in
respecting me before you kissed me I thought
would carry over to sex; but instead,
it's treated like an insignificant milestone,

a notch in your sexuality, an aside.
Now a part of me no longer believes you
are different;
that sex was the
end goal of your agenda
the whole time. That maybe, that was
the only part of
your agenda. That maybe,
men never prove me wrong.
I am distraught at my
sudden mistrust in you.
I am conflicted.
One, two, three chances and I will begin to
close my door. And I
am afraid that once I
close it, I will not
come back.

October 18th
No matter how many times I
wash my hands, I just can't seem to
rid myself of your scent. I breathe
into my fingers and
inhale the essence that reminds me of
running my palms through your hair,
the smell of your skin
pressed into mine, and the
soft line of your shirt
nudging your collar bone.
You smell like masculinity; the kind that I
fear might overpower me
then eventually leave me
without looking back.
You linger within the
vacant slots between my fingertips,
flooding my senses with the
memories of

you I will never get back.
Your hands leave mine and my
heart feels like the hollow
spaces your fingers were meant to fill,
and I feel nothing
but (

)
emptiness.

upon dilemma
Moving to Washington D.C.
to work on
the 2016 presidential campaign is
a once-in-a-lifetime opportunity
but so is
being with me.

October 19th
Your embraces comfort me like linens fresh
out the dryer, the kinds that
clothe my body in heat as I
lay in my clean covers and
inhale
into nostalgia.

Your embraces calm me like hot bath water, running over my naked legs, melting my distress, steaming my skin red as my sweat evaporates into relief.

Your embraces envelop me like the soft,
pink flesh of a clam that
protects a pearl, cloaking the treasure of
its most precious, opalescent possession,
hiding it from the bitterness of
the world, hoping to never let go. And I
pray that you never let go, because I'm
going to miss them
when they're gone.

October 23rd

I am cherishing my last
everything with you.
I am cherishing our last date, the last
time we walk hand in hand in the
moonlight, and it's devastating that you
had a cold sore and couldn't
kiss me because I
would have kissed you knowing I
never will again.
I am cherishing our last embrace,
the kind where you
press your whole body against mine and
the heat that emanates from within you
melts the frigidity of my heart and
pushes out the
depravity from inside.
I am cherishing the last time you
place your head to my breast
and listen to my heartbeat,
reassuring yourself that I
have one in the first place, and I am afraid
it will stop beating when you leave.

I am cherishing the last time you
run your hand down my thighs and
press your lips against them and sigh like
my skin is the softest thing
you've ever tasted.

I am cherishing the last time you
cup my left breast softly with
your palm, like holding a fresh
baby bird, dreading the day
it will fly away.
I am cherishing the last time you

look at me with dilated pupils,
all the while thinking,
Damn, this girl is mine.
Because I was yours,
and I'm afraid I still am
and will be
for a long time
after you're gone.

The end
I cannot stop writing
about you without
seeing the end of everything.

October 26th
I spent a decade
building a fortress around my heart,
to protect myself from the pain
inflicted from
outside invaders
till one day I
realized it was awfully lonely in this
lofty castle I had built for
myself

because
the only one inside
was me.

upon self-destruction
This love is entropy.
I can feel it take hold like
verdant plant roots take hold of the
grainy concrete block that constitutes my
heart, and it crumbles under the weight of
the lush, twisted branches that wrap around it
disintegrating, and I am afraid I
won't be able to pick up the pieces when
you're gone.
This love is madness.
I can feel it mess with my mind like
the kind of insanity that requires lethal
injection and ominous last words recorded,
because who said love wasn't
admissible lunacy anyways?
25

This love is poison.
I can feel it sickening me like
streaks of venom shooting out from
violent spider bites scratched out, festering
puss that oozes down the side of my leg,
all the while afraid that you
might be the cure.
This love is a drug.
I can feel it rushing over me like
uncontrollable toxins that trick

neurotransmitters and overwhelm me until I

**am crashing down crescent slopes,
all the while afraid that
you are the antidrug.**

October 28th
Ten years of loneliness was
less painful than
letting you
into my life.
Ten years of loneliness was
less painful than you
leaving me to
move to Washington D.C.
Ten years of loneliness was
less painful than you
telling me you
needed more time to
fall in love with me.
But ten years of loneliness wasn't
worth it like it was
trying to love you.

October 29th
Maybe love is
a lose-lose game, since
we place ourselves in someone else and
when they leave our
souls are sucked out like
wisps of frozen breaths
that evaporate in the black
vacancy of the nighttime and our
lungs are left
gasping for air.

the winter
It will feel colder in California when
you come back but I'm
afraid I
won't be here to
keep you warm.

October 30th
Before you came along I
was a crumpled piece of paper but your
lack of words flattened me and now
I'm left numb and lackluster.

upon saying thank you

You swallow your words like
they're pellets of poison that you're
afraid will hurt me once
they hit my ears and
lodge a bullet hole in my heart but
instead they're stuck in your throat
slowly suffocating you and as you
begin to decay you
watch me disintegrate in front of
your ice-cold eyes

**because the very words you
never let escape your
lips were the ones my
lungs needed to breathe,**
and instead we're both
left choking to death.

upon silence

I never imagined that
the words that would hurt me the most
would be the ones
you never spoke.

November 1st

Your silence was a knife that
pierced my heart multiple times and
left me bleeding amidst all
your unspoken words.

upon regret

If I could press delete on
our relationship I would;
turn back the dial and erase
all the places your hands touched me
and brought me shame when you
pulled me so close I
thought I would break and now
it pains me to realize that you
used me to make yourself
feel better.

November 2ⁿᵈ

The silence you gave me was
colder than any winter I
have ever experienced.

upon letting go

When I think about you now I
like to think about the
first time you held my hand
gently, with three fingers because you
were afraid to show
your friends you liked me but you
also couldn't let go. I
smile not because I
miss you but because that
was the most
genuine moment
we shared.

November 3ʳᵈ

I knew I was over you the moment I
realized you had
stolen my smile for weeks and I
no longer resented you; but rather,
pitied you for

29

darkening the universe,
eclipsing me, who you
kept hidden for yourself
under your dank, dark clouds that
forced me inside, cold and wet and
alone for months.

upon frowning
Anybody that steals your smile
for weeks
doesn't deserve your love,
because essentially what they're doing is
dimming the world by
trying to
blot out your sunshine.

Fuck boys.
Fuck.
boys.
Fuck boys that look at you
blankly with their hefty, ignorant eyes
when you
tell them you love them
and they
have nothing to say in return.
Fuck boys that steal your smile for weeks,
because the world deserves to experience
your love.
Fuck boys that diminish your spirit,
that tarnish you,
that pull down and press you.
Fuck boys that try to dampen you.

upon inspiration
You came, conquered,
stole my heart and
left me with a Moleskin full of
pensive poems documenting unrequited love
exposed on cream, lined pages.

November 5th
You should have said
nothing to me and
walked away as opposed to
holding hypothetical information about
your feelings
over my head like I
was a yo-yo you
were playing with
and your tailored words the string you
wanted to keep me on.

November 9th
What do you do,
when you don't know what to do,
when you can't breathe,
inhaling: *I want to, I want to, I want to,*
try.
Exhaling: *I can't, I can't, I can't*
do it.
Choking on gasps of air,
brain tormented by *it's too much,*
it's too painful trying to love you,
trying to figure out if
you love me too.

repression
Acrylic on canvas

32

upon finding out she was dying
Everything is broken.
My heart pulled apart in
three pieces, tugged in three directions
drawn and quartered till
the portions bleed,
lying bare-naked on the floor,
separated,
all beating distinct heartbeats,
which keep slowing down
till the dark, ominous silence
overwhelms the street onlookers
viewing this massacre
in the street and they
realize the radiating pulses have stopped
simultaneously and I
have stopped living.

November 12th
I can see the words
coming out of my mouth
like vomit
but I can't stop them.
Swallowing pain like pills
over and over again,
regurgitating torment
trying so hard not to
get intoxicated off of your sight
swallowing deeply of
the look in your eyes
getting tipsy on
the moons of your black pupils
feeling high off your presence
sensing that upward rush of ecstasy
then that catastrophic decline,
crashing into dismal voids
like a depressant

where I realize your
toxins have overtaken me and my
heart has to be pumped dry because

I am drunk on you.

November 14th
*upon my brother-in-law telling me
he didn't want to be a single dad*
Tell the people you love that
you love them, hold them
close to you, and
cherish them because
life is short.

The above statement is
considered cliché.
It's considered cliché until we
face the harsh, abrupt
reality of the sheer temporal nature
of this life and then it
becomes *the only thing
that actually matters.*

November 16ᵗʰ

I have a feeling I'm going to know you
for a long time, he told me when he
left me, eyes never looking at me,
turned away like folding the corners
of books, to be picked up again
years later
or maybe never.
Why? I asked, my throat croaking;
dry with doubt, as if I had swallowed
a cluster of cotton balls soaked
in the fluid of my blackest fears.
Because I want to, he tried to
reassure me.
But when I told him
my sister was dying, stage 4 cancer
deteriorating her bones—terminal—he told me

he couldn't spend time with me
because he was too busy
writing an essay.

Maybe you want more time alone now
anyways, I don't know, he told me.
I don't know.
I don't know how to answer two of
life's most profound mysteries—
why we adamantly love those
that treat us with contempt
while those that adore us
get taken from us
abruptly,
and unexpectedly
as if they were never here in the first place.

November 17th

In how many different ways can
you break my heart?

First, you crushed it;
ground it into tiny little pieces
and I used my tears and love to
make a paste out of it,
remolded it into a heartbeat,
bursting forth of forgiveness.

Then you flattened it;
rolled it out with a pin
and snipped it with scissors
to make a cake out of it,
cut and splattered, cooking in the oven
of your puffed up promises and
faulty reassurances—lies.
Then you took a bite out of it
and it went down sweet till
you spit it back in my face,
regurgitated vomit; bitter,
processed, digested, and rejected,
pulverized to a powder
that you threw up into the air with
your hands so it would
get lost in the wind and I
wouldn't be able to
put it back together again.

December 10th
What Christmas present
do you buy for someone who's dying?
Do you buy them a coffin, or
do you buy yourself one too
because you also
want to curl up in a ball
and die?

December 11th
Before I kissed him, I
told him I had been
running from relationships for ten years;
my heart broken over and over again from
unrequited loves.
I'm gonna help you through that,
he promised me.
But then when he finally got over me, I
looked at the emptiness in his expression,
devoid of any feeling for me
and I knew he
didn't love me
never loved me
and that's when I vowed he would be
my last unrequited love.

37

December 13th
I need to get away from
everything that reminds me of you.
Not because I don't love you; but rather,
because I do too much and
it's suffocating me.
You're the first thing I think of when I
wake up in the morning and my
last thought before I go to sleep;
going crazy.
Thoughts lack clarity.
It's hazy.

You've colonized my mind and I want to slice out different sections of my brain just to stop thinking about you

because this is madness.
You're not leaving and I
feel like a piece of trash
you discarded because I
was no longer convenient to you.
Already, I've cried a trillion tears
over you and I
just don't know how many more times
you can break my heart.
I can't save you and
save myself too.

In trying to preserve this, I've lost myself and in order to regain me I have to discard you too.

December 15th
I don't wear my heart on my sleeve.
I hide it, tucked away underneath my
right breast and that's why I
didn't want you to
touch me there
at first.
I tried desperately to
harbor it from you; but then,
lost it from me.
We fell deeper and
somehow swimming in
your ocean gasping for air, I
forfeited it and
you found it

**drowning in the murky waters of
bruised expectations,
crushed underneath the weight of
your failings,**
I waited for you to
give it mouth to mouth
resuscitation
but instead it
slipped from your fish fingers
and its dying heartbeats
created the last ripple waves
across the puddle of our
deceased love,
liquidated
as it sank to the bottom
like a stone,
fossilized black,
existing only as a remnant of the past,
mythical,
and never to be seen again.

39

December 21st

Our love began during the year of
California's record drought.
Then I ended it a day before
your graduation and it
rained torrentially.
Just like my tears.

And I breathed a sigh of relief because it was over.

The aftermath.

For crying girls everywhere,
hiding in the bathroom stall.
May you find your healing.

upon diluting myself
I am a woman.
I dilute myself in order to survive;
I suppress myself, recoiling into a tight ball
to not threaten the *more powerful* sex
so they don't realize that
the most beautiful part of me is
my brain and not my body,
my thoughts and not my tits,
my heart and not my hair,
my feelings and not my face.
I am a woman.
I diminish myself in order to survive;
I demean myself;
I'm not true to myself;
but as I grow smaller I
actually grow bigger
because I am developing something that men
cannot, not having to learn how to navigate,
how to cope
in this male-dominated labyrinth
where penises
call the shots,
trying to make it out scathe free
without being raped, abused, threatened,
assaulted, harassed, ogled at, kidnapped,
stalked, sexualized, grabbed, fingered,
manipulated, demeaned, tortured, killed.
I am a woman.
I am learning resiliency.
This is why women survive.

living longer than men, bearing children,
raising families alone, recovering from abuse,
healing as they
heal others.
Nurturing those around them
as they themselves suffer from
emotional nutrient deficiency.
I am a woman.
I swallow come-ons like candy,
sexism poisoning
my stomach lining like pills,
my body bearing cavities from
years of abuse
on the streets, in the home, in the bedroom.
I am a woman.
I regurgitate bitter smiles, verbal hedges,
pervasive suspicion, socialized distrust,
knuckles locked on pepper spray bottles,
brisk walks through dark alleys holding keys,
trained silence,
learned indifference.

I am a woman,
and I am in need of a deep root canal,
but I'm afraid the dentist is out of business.

February 12ᵗʰ
men make me feel uncomfortable
My beauty makes men
feel comfortable with me.
Too fast,
in a forward fashion.
They sit close to me on
public transportation full of vacant seats.
Elderly men like to
look at me,
gazing,

they call me beautiful and
rub my hand
like we're best friends,
but we're not.
Men of all sorts make me feel unsafe.
They lean over and touch my thigh,
sweating palms running across
the bare two inches of skin
in between the hem of my skirt
and the tops of my socks.
I begin to question
my choice of lipstick
or the lack of fabric over my
two inches of naked leg.
I begin to question my beauty.
But then I realize
the irony is that
it makes men feel comfortable,
as men make me feel
deathly uncomfortable.

upon walking down the street
UC Berkeley needs to cool it down
with the construction—not because of
the noise, the smell, or the blatant
inconvenience when walking; but rather,
because only by walking
to the bus stop on Southside I pass by
three construction crews, on a daily basis.
All eating their lunches,
who stop simultaneously to watch
me walk from one corner of the
block to the other, leering, as if
they've never seen a woman before, as if
my existence was solely for
their viewing pleasure. As if
the entire sum of my being as a

43

human was my breasts, legs and ass.

Y cuando me refieren en español puedo entenderlos, desafortunadamente para mis orejas y mi corazón.
But on a lucky day, I am forced to
plug my ears and lower my lids
and protectively disregard all
such unbridled behaviors, and
everyday my soul shrinks a little more,
as I walk by, until slowly it
crumbles into oblivion.

upon being a woman
Curtis:
talks smooth game about
wanting to cuddle
but I don't want him to
touch me.
He grabs my arm on my
best friend's couch
and claws towards my
breast. I fling
him off.
I am twenty-six;
about to turn twenty-seven.
men never prove me wrong.
An elderly man:
sits too close to me
on the bus
again
where there are
rows of empty seats.
He rubs the two inches of
bare skin on my thigh,
the one in between my
socks and my skirt.

I like the color of your skin,
he tells me.
I flinch but
don't say anything.
I am twenty-five.
men never prove me wrong.
A group of men:
proceed to grab my butt
under my skirt as I
walk down the street
with some friends.
No matter that I was
walking with two male
acquaintances.
Josh: I'm afraid to
date him, who,
despite being
my best friend and perhaps a
bigger feminist than
me, might still pressure me to
have sex with him
too soon.
men never prove me wrong.
I am twenty-four.
Micah:
turns to me in friendly Spanish
conversation y me pregunta,
queires hacer el amor?
y yo no tengo las palabras
para refutarlo.
Tengo veinticuatro años.
los hombres nunca me proban errada.
Lucas:
an older (married) male coworker, is fired
for sexually harassing me
and my other female coworker;
nine months after the fact.

I am twenty-three.
men never prove me wrong.
Bruce:
comes home drunk one night
and asks me to
strip for him on the pole.
Even after refusing
multiple times, he persists.
Why not?
he keeps on
repeating to me.
A drunk man:
in a dark alley in the city
solicits my best friend and me
for oral sex. When we refuse,
he follows after us
calling, *but I have a big dick!*
Can I have a blow job?
We are horrified.
I am twenty-three.
men never prove me wrong.
An older man:
stops me on campus to ask
if he can take photos of me
for his portfolio.
Why not? he asks me
multiple times when I refuse;
You're tall and beautiful, he assures me.
I am twenty-two.
men never prove me wrong.
The words of
the construction workers:
fixing my mother's house
stop me on my way to work, as I've
finally begun to understand in Spanish
what they say about my body as I saunter
past them every morning.

Their gazes following me
as I retreat to my car y
trato de no escucharlos.
Tengo veintiuno años.
los hombres nunca me proban errada.
A homeless man:
asks to sit next to me
and I
don't want to say no because
he is black,
I want to say no because
he is a man.
So he,
sits next to me at In n Out and
masturbates as
he watches me
masticate a
burger. The restaurant calls
the cops and I run away
to my car.
I am twenty.
men never prove me wrong.
Men:
consistently stop to
talk to me, commenting on my
appearance, and coming on to me while
I read at cafés.
While mentoring high school
girls, a man approaches me and
proceeds to hit on me
in front of them.
I want to be left alone; I
want him to leave them alone.
I am nineteen.
men never prove me wrong.
Older men:
sit next to me on the bus

too close,
they ask me when and where
they can see me again.
I am eighteen.
men never prove me wrong.
More older men:
stop me on the street
on my way home from school,
telling me how *gorgeous* I am,
and that I am the *most beautiful woman*
they have ever seen.
On a good day, I don't
get followed to work.
I am seventeen.
men never prove me wrong.
Derrick:
persistently follows me around
school, town, and to
church professing his love for
me and reading the love poems he
writes about me
to my friends. I don't remember
how many times
I try to run
away.
I am sixteen.
men never prove me wrong.

I pray God will
forgive me for letting
Andrew touch me.

I am fifteen years old.
men never prove me wrong.
Thirty-year old men:
message me on
Myspace, telling me how
pretty I am, and what they

want to do to my body.
I am fourteen.
men never prove me wrong.
My best friend Jacob:
falls in love with me and
threatens to
commit suicide
because I don't
like him back.
I am thirteen.
men never prove me wrong.
I pray God will
forgive me for letting
Andrew touch me.
I am ten years old.
men never prove me wrong.
Andrew:
frequently beats me at
Sonic the Hedgehog on the Nintendo so
he could take me in the back room and
finger me as a prize.
Every time I lose, he
makes me take off my underwear and
feel around, and then have me mirror
the actions
on him.
He makes me do this
multiple times. I've never felt
more ashamed.

**To this day, I've
never repeated that
story to anyone.
I am seven.**
men never prove me wrong.
Jeremy:

tries to kiss me.
He follows me after
school, and behind a tree tries to plant
one on my lips. He misses and lands
on my neck—right on my collar bone.
I run the rest of the way home.
I am five.
men never prove me wrong.

Prove me wrong.

February 15th
do they make makeup for crying girls?
Do they make makeup for crying girls?
The kind of mascara I can
wear to my sister's funeral,
where I don't have to fear

**the black tracks running down
the smooth skin of my
cheeks, marking the years I
will spend crying for her absence.**

Do they make makeup for crying girls?
The kind of lipstick that doesn't
leave crimson smudges across
my mouth and
the back of my hand as I
wipe tears shed over
all the men that
didn't love me back.

Do they make makeup for crying girls?
The kind of blush that
doesn't bleach lines of
negative space down my cheeks,

the kind of makeup sold for girls who
were sexually assaulted at seven years old,
triggered by a poem on *Huffington Post*

as she remembers how
his fingers felt inside her.

The kind of makeup sold for girls
who cry for their friends
as they leave her one by one,
and she's left alone in her bedroom,
clutching her pillows,
drowning in swimming pools.

Maybe they sell something at the store that
makes a black heart pretty,
that covers up the pain and scars
in artificial pigments.

But they don't sell cover up for the heart,
and even if they did it'd still be
the same superficial shit they sell to
make girls look like they haven't been
crying in the bathroom stall,
flushing the toilet so the other
crying girl next to her
won't hear.

So for now I'll resort to
wearing the same makeup they sell
to happy girls faking their glee
in shades of nude and fuchsia
walking down the street with
fake smiles drawn on their faces
pretending not to be a
crying girl because the world
tells them that girls are

51

too pretty to cry,
too beautiful not to smile,
and because they
don't make makeup for
crying girls.

December – February
upon watching her die in front of me
I keep my challenges to myself.
On the inside,
the cavity of my body
painted in
silent crises.
On the outside,
my lips painted red in
an upturned pout
masquerading as a smile.
My hair tied up in
a gray ribbon
reflecting the aesthetic of
my turmoiled intestines,
and everyone is unaware that

*I am pregnant with a conflict,
swollen in vicissitude
and I'm afraid I have
miscarried all the remnants
of hope.*

February 16th

upon dreaming about her

The separation between heaven and earth is a border

and I don't have
citizenship yet.

February 23rd

upon experiencing ptsd

The pupils of cancer, death-ridden,
doped up on drugs
and small with flecks
of gold and green,
as the last bits of
sanity slips from her fingertips.

March 3rd

My spirit was a
broken bulb that they
put in the ground,
but when it
didn't grow they:
scolded it,
dismissed it,
shamed it;
little did they know that
you need to water spirits
in order for them
to grow.
But they let it sink there,
sifting,
dry as a bone because
there's a shortage of
gardeners who know how to

53

resuscitate spirits buried in a cemetery
during a drought.

March 10th
One death sets off
another death;
A Rube Goldberg
machine about deaths.

March 15th
We're both stuck on
different rooftops,
looking at
the same sunset.

upon inheritance
They ask me
where I got my
coats from, my
purses from, my
boots from and
I reply with
waterfalls cascading from my
skull: *I got them from*
my sister.
They're beautiful, they
tell me and I
walk away with
gushing rivers leaking upon
her coat,
her purse,
her boots, because her clothes
are just an empty shell
that once clothed a soul,
who I miss, that

no longer needs
outer garments to
cover her in
forever sleep.

April 11th
I live in the expectations I
have built.
I huddle under their rooftops,
clutching;
longing, hoping, wishing for
things that won't ever happen.
I try to leave them but
I don't
know how.

I made a little house for you in my head and let you live there. *But you don't even pay fucking rent.*

I tried to evict you
and you left but
came back knocking on
the door of these erected expectations
I have built
for myself
and for you.
Then we both got lost
trying to navigate
the labyrinth of deferred hope,
trying to understand
what we currently are or
what we have left
and we
might not make it out again.
55

June 10th
I wear my brokenness like
a window cracked in winter,
erect;
within the wooden frame,
a crystalline snowflake that
one mistakes for an art piece.

how do you perform CPR on a broken heart?
———————***can you?***
You bear the breasts,
then take your left hand and
place it between them,
interlocking fingers pressing down
through already cracked cartilage
to feel the shards of
brokenness underneath,
stick to fingertips as you lift up;
the pieces blow away in the wind
and you lose the last remnants
of the broken heart
till all that's left is
an empty cavity
and your last hope is to
perform mouth-to-mouth
in a final attempt to resuscitate
prior to the

———————————**flatline**

_____

————————————.

upon celebrating international women's day
I love how we (womankind)
get one day a year to
honor womanhood
and the rest of the time men
are busy getting paid
more than us,
getting recognized
more than us,
having their voice heard,
more than us.
I love how
the rest of the 364 days that
are men's day they're busy
running the world and
fucking it up.
Well, *mazel tov*
and
good luck to them.

upon being a woman (reprise)
I'm finished.
Long past traumatized;
post-traumatized.
because
men never prove me wrong.
I feel
residual grief.
Exhausted from
continually
spurning male
advances
towards me,
and others.
The number of unsolicited
looks, comments, threatening advances,
and nonconsensual touches

I've received over the
course of my very short life
I can't count.
men never prove me wrong.
men never prove us wrong
(but I want them to).
And I always give them chances,
but I'm running out of
steam.

Prove me wrong.
Please.

here's to the woman
One day in the year cannot
truly honor and recognize the amount of
unappreciated work that women
actually contribute to the world.
But we can try, so,
here's to the woman:
Here's to the single mother
working 1+ jobs to support her family;
Here's to the woman pioneering
in a male-dominated field
while facing discrimination,
belittlement and/or harassment
and still shows up;
Here's to the woman who
gave up a career to raise her children;
Here's to the woman who
put off starting a family
to pursue a career;
Here's to the grandmother raising
her grandchildren in retirement;
Here's to the mother who
left everything in her home country to
provide a better life for her children;

Here's to the sexual assault survivor who's
asked, *but what were you wearing?*
Here's to the woman who
pursues an education—despite the
physical danger it may put her in;
Here's to the woman who's
told she's not
pretty enough
she wasn't asking you;
Here's to the woman who's
told she's *too* pretty *to do that—*
but does it anyway.
Here's to the woman who
speaks out against sexism
while being challenged
and still speaks;

**Here's to the woman whose
societal contributions are overlooked
because she was not born a man.
Here's to the woman.**

Thank you.

autobiography
Acrylic on canvas

Acknowledgments

I am truly honored, humbled and indebted to all the magnificent women that contributed to this creative endeavor. First, thank you to Gretchen Tolentino for telling me to publish this body of work. Infinite thanks to my editor and greatest fan: Maria Ciccone. Thank you for reviewing each draft, and for believing in my voice. Thank you to Iris Lopez for perfecting my Spanish lines. Lastly, thank you to Arielle Anthony for paving the way for me to write poetry and for giving me the courage to be my truest self.

Biography

Emmanuella Hristova was born in Oakland, California and grew up in the Bay Area. She is the third daughter to Bulgarian parents who immigrated to California shortly before she was born. She began drawing at the ripe age of four and studied the fine arts for five years in high school. There, she received many art accolades including a Congressional award for her piece *Boy in Red* in 2009. In 2015, she received her Bachelor of Arts in Linguistics from the University of California, Berkeley. She began writing poetry at age twenty-four when she was in graduate school. She earned her Master's in Education from the same alma mater in 2017. Emmanuella spent two years as an English teacher in Richmond, California. During that time, she self-published her first poetry collection: *The Day My Kisses Tasted Like Disorder*. Her poems have been published in independent literature magazines and *365 Days of Covid*, a poetry anthology. Currently, she is writing her second novel while seeking literary representation for her first. She speaks English, Bulgarian, Spanish and now resides in Paris, France where she is teaching English and learning French.

www.ehristova.com

@emmy_speaks

ehristova.com

@emmy_speaks

www.ingramcontent.com/pod-product-compliance
Lightning Source LLC
Chambersburg PA
CBHW041104110426
42740CB00043B/152